BACK OFF! ANIMAL DEFENSES
ELECTRIC ANIMALS

by Cari Meister

Ideas for Parents and Teachers

Pogo Books let children practice reading informational text while introducing them to nonfiction features such as headings, labels, sidebars, maps, and diagrams, as well as a table of contents, glossary, and index.

Carefully leveled text with a strong photo match offers early fluent readers the support they need to succeed.

Before Reading

• "Walk" through the book and point out the various nonfiction features. Ask the student what purpose each feature serves.

• Look at the glossary together. Read and discuss the words.

Read the Book

• Have the child read the book independently.

• Invite him or her to list questions that arise from reading.

After Reading

• Discuss the child's questions. Talk about how he or she might find answers to those questions.

• Prompt the child to think more. Ask: Have you seen any of the electric animals mentioned in the book? Can you think of any electric animals that aren't discussed?

Pogo Books are published by Jump!
5357 Penn Avenue South
Minneapolis, MN 55419
www.jumplibrary.com

Library of Congress Cataloging-in-Publication Data

Meister, Cari, author.
  Electric animals / by Cari Meister.
      pages cm. – (Back off! Animal defenses)
  Audience: Ages 7-10.
  Summary: "Carefully leveled text and vibrant photographs introduce readers to electric animals such as the stargazer, torpedo ray, electric eel, and explore how they use electricity to defend themselves against predators. Includes activity, glossary, and index."–Provided by publisher.
  Includes bibliographical references and index.
  ISBN 978-1-62031-309-1 (hardcover: alk. paper) – ISBN 978-1-62496-375-9 (ebook)
  1. Animal defenses–Juvenile literature.
  2. Animal weapons–Juvenile literature.
  3. Electrophysiology–Juvenile literature.
  4. Electric fishes–Juvenile literature. I. Title.
  QL759.M455 2016
  591.47–dc23
                                    2015034814

Series Editor: Jenny Fretland VanVoorst
Series Designer: Anna Peterson
Book Designer: Ellen Schofield
Photo Researcher: Jenny Fretland VanVoorst

Photo Credits: Alamy, 1, 4, 13, 14-15, 20-21; Sea Pics, cover; SuperStock, 5, 8-9, 10, 12-13, 17, 18-19; Shutterstock, 3, 8-9, 11; Thinkstock, 6-7, 16, 23.

Printed in the United States of America at Corporate Graphics in North Mankato, Minnesota.

TABLE OF CONTENTS

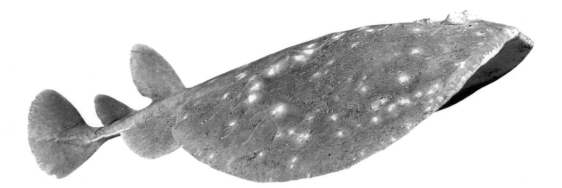

CHAPTER 1

· ·

ZAPPING EYES

What is that hiding
on the ocean floor?

A stargazer fish!
This fish uses its fins to
bury itself in the sand.

Do you see its eyes? They move in circles. That's not the only cool thing they do. They also zap **electricity**!

A shark swims by. He wants to eat the fish. Think again, Mr. Shark! The fish zaps the shark. The shark is shocked. He swims away.

A stargazer's zap is not very strong, but it does send a warning. Stay away from me!

··

CHAPTER 2

FLABBY ZAPPERS

This flabby tough guy does not have many **predators**. After all, who wants to be zapped while eating?

Torpedo rays mostly use their zapping powers on **prey**. However, if they are scared, they will show their stuff!

prey
(garden eel)

Rays can make **electrical charges** whenever they want. They can also control how much power goes into each zap.

Rays have special muscle tissues that create power. The tissues are in two **glands**. The glands are huge! They look like big kidneys.

electrical glands

Many rays have zapping powers.
But torpedo rays win the
"Most Powerful Ray" award.
They can jolt up to 50 volts!
That is not enough power
to kill a person, but it can
knock someone out.

DID YOU KNOW?

Ancient Greeks used
electric fish in operations.
Doctors used them to
numb an area before
they cut.

CHAPTER 3

· ·

POWER ZAPPER

An eel swims in the Amazon River. He has no enemies.

Wait! What's this? A **caiman**! The eel doesn't take chances. He sends off an electrical charge. Zap! It shocks the caiman. She swims away.

Eels have 6,000 **electrocytes** on their bodies. These are cells. They act like batteries. They store power. When an eel is spooked, the power turns on.

How does an electric eel compare with some electrical devices? Let's see.

VOLTS

50,000

TASER
50,000 volts

5,000

ELECTRIC FENCE FOR LIVESTOCK
3,000–5,000 volts

600

ELECTRIC EEL
Up to 600 volts

110

LIGHT SOCKET
110 volts

0

The shock from an eel does not kill a person. It can make someone stop breathing. It can also make someone have a heart attack. Some people die when shocked because they drown.

DID YOU KNOW?

A mall in Japan had a Christmas tree powered by an eel. Every time the eel moved, the lights went on. It makes you wonder: What else can an eel power?

ACTIVITIES & TOOLS

TRY THIS!

STATIC ELECTRICITY

You can zap your friends with a harmless static charge in this simple activity.

You will need:
- a carpeted room
- socks
- a friend

Steps:

1. Put on your socks.

2. Slide or shuffle your feet around the carpeted room. This builds up static electricity.

3. Touch your friend's skin.

4. Zap!

5. If you have several friends, try a game of electric eel zapping tag.

caiman: A reptile similar to a crocodile.

electrical charges: Pulses of energy.

electricity: A form of energy.

electrocytes: Muscle-like cells that can produce volts.

glands: An organ in the body that makes something.

predators: An animal that hunts other animals for food.

prey: An animal that is hunted for food.

TO LEARN MORE

Learning more is as easy as 1, 2, 3.

1) Go to www.factsurfer.com

2) Enter "electricanimals" into the search box.

3) Click the "Surf" button to see a list of websites.

With factsurfer, finding more information is just a click away.